YOU KNOW YOU'RE A NEVADAN IF ...

Written by Guy Clifton
Writer and Columnist for the Reno Gazette-Journal
including contributions from Reno Gazette-Journal readers
Illustrated by Marilyn Melton
Introduction by Governor Kenny Guinn

Nevada Humanities Committee • 2002

NEVADA
HUMANITIES
COMMITTEE

Cover:

☐　　You remember when there was diagonal parking on Virginia St. in Reno.

A Halcyon imprint of the Nevada Humanities Committee

ISBN 1-890591-13-0

Nevada Humanities Committee
P.O. Box 8029
Reno, NV 89507

Dedicated to all those who know the proper way to pronounce Nevada.

My thanks to the following people for all their help with picture research
• Nancy Spina
• Jeannie Rasmussen
• Neal Cobb
• the staff at the Nevada Historical Society
• Mae Franco
• Lenita Powers

Marilyn Melton

Thank you to all the *Reno Gazette-Journal* readers/contributors to this book. Please see a list on page 4.

My gratitude goes to:
* John Trent and Kim Foster, who helped develop the idea for this book while dipping their pizza crust in honey at JJ's Pie Company — a sure sign they must be Nevadans.
* Marilyn Melton, who brings words to life with her illustrations.
* Judith Winzeler and the Nevada Humanities Committee.
* Gov. Kenny Guinn, Mike O'Callaghan, Sam Dibitonto, John L. Smith and Richard Bryan for their contributions.
* Miller and Lorraine Clifton for moving the family across the country and making Nevada our home.

Guy Clifton

Thank you to the following people for contributions to this book:
Heather Flowers, Kim Pisane, Tori Bowlin, Greg Bortolin, Natalie Warstler, Kelli Du Fresne,
Amanda Hammon, Mick Laxalt, Chet Piazzo, Sam Dibitonto, Jason Geddes, Sharon Nickson Cox,
Gary McCuin, Steve Martarano, Billy Vance, Peggy Hannah, Annie Hellmann, Kirk Kelsie, Amy Peterson,
Robert Lee, Kelly Fassett, Alan Hopper, Royce Feour, Bryan Allison, Dawn Green, Treva Lind,
Bob Weyer, Lois Boudwin, Jean Hubbard, Steve McPartland, Sharon Saal, Kim Kaiser, Kristin McQueary,
Gary Dyer, Link Piazzo, Dick Trachok, Bill Cobb, Norma Scott, Nevada Lambert, Debra Rilea,
Teresa West, Warren Mouser, Don Stephens, Sylvia Kurzrock, John Potter, Rick & Linda Reinick,
Dick Gammick, Norma Gregory, Kathy Hannah, Jean Stoess, Deanna Ashby,
Rick & Jane (Eliades) Davidsaver, Steve Ball, Ed Hewitt, Guy Rocha, Andy Barbarno, Neal Cobb,
Maizie Harris Jesse, Alan Mela, John Trent, Timothy Jay, Dianne Headen, Mike Hamilton, Betty Glass,
Lisa & Bill Groom, Vern Austin, Russ Schooley, Tom & Phyllis Cates, Dan Williams, Wayne Pearson,
Ken Hummel, Don "Snoshu" Thompson, Leo Horishny, Ray Hagar, Dick Colon, Joe & Nan Martin,
Joe Altick, Denise Drakulich Altick, Timothy Ennor, Steve Anderson, Joan Johnson, Leslie Frey,
Shari Mogensen, Jim Bauer, Len Crocker, Roz Parry, Julie Johnson, John Fisher,
Steve & Sandy Johnson, Jim Rogers, Mike & Marie Affinito, Joye Reeder, Bruno Buonanoma,
Darlene Look, Neil Brooks, Morrey Troutner, Karmen Ferris, Candace Dean Silveria, Gordon Foote,
Faye Mariluch, John Slansky, Guy W. Farmer, Elwood Hill, Paula A. Crider, Peter P. Papadakos,
Dave Quandt, Nancy Humphries, Jim & Laura Casson, Tony P. Limon, Bob Smith, Cameron Sydenham,
John Lengel, Les McKenzie, Austin Wilson, Al Saibini, Sunny Allen, Bill Crosswhite, Larry Schultze,
Gregg Zive, Joanne Murray, Joe Peroglio, Cliff Weaver, Diane Carlin, Carl G. Looney, Marie Werner,
Francis Trigero, Stephanie & Larry Moen, Chuck Hildebrand, Jerry Schultz, Elizabeth Brady,
Jan Edwards, Len Trout III, Patrick Deming, Jerry & Carole Gribble, Jan Bunning, Sheila Wimer,
Ellen Fockler, Jeannie Cassinellli, Tim Fitzpatrick, Michael Sanderson, John Deming, Penny Landell
Getts, Marjorie Simon Tavernia, Hank Garell, Paul Kincade, Phyllis Mathews, Pauline Carpenter,
Aubrey L. Keen, Fred Sanford, Terri Hickey, Edward C. Tyson, Sharon Genung, Holly O'Driscoll,
Gary Lubra, and Mamie Deckwa.

Preface

Last fall, as a tribute to Nevada Day, I thought it might be fun to try to figure out what defines a Nevadan. The 2000 Census revealed that the Silver State has the least number of natives of any state in the Union.

I have to admit, I'm not a native myself. The Cliftons moved to Nevada in 1964 when I was 2. In the 38 years that have followed, though, I've never considered myself anything but a Nevadan. I think, like a lot of people, I've always considered being a Nevadan more of an attitude than a birthright.

So I wrote a column with the headline, "Signs you might be a Nevadan." It listed a handful of items I thought only true Nevadans would know — things like "you've thrown a rock down a mine shaft," and "you know Governor Mike." I thought people might get a chuckle. Maybe a reader or two would send in a response.

I never expected the hundreds of e-mails, phone calls and letters that followed. They came in waves and continued, not for days, but for weeks and months. A year later, I still receive submissions every week from people who run across the original column on the Internet.

The majority of correspondence came from people still living in the Silver State, but there were dozens from displaced Nevadans living elsewhere — New Jersey, Virginia, Louisiana, Texas, Utah, Washington, Oregon and California. One e-mail came from Singapore, another from London. But perhaps the most touching came from the aircraft carrier USS Theodore Roosevelt, the command ship for Operation Enduring Freedom, which was stationed in the Arabian Gulf at the time. Winnemucca's Dawn Green, a Navy senior chief, e-mailed to say thank you for a single item: "You love the smell of sagebrush in the rain."

My hope for this book is that these items spark a pleasant memory, bring a smile and remind us that, no matter where we live, Nevada will always be home.

Guy Clifton

Introduction
Governor Kenny Guinn

Although home has meant Las Vegas for Dema and me for more than 38 years, we consider all of Nevada to be our home, especially since I became Governor four years ago.

While the vast majority of us live in either Las Vegas or Reno, there is much more to being a Nevadan than working in one of the world-class resorts on the Strip or skiing on a mountain with a breathtaking view of Lake Tahoe, that Mark Twain once described as the fairest picture the whole earth affords.

Nevadans are a proud people, proud of their heritage, proud of their wide-open spaces and proud of where they work. The late great Nevada author Robert Laxalt came as close to anyone I have ever heard define the Nevada spirit when he wrote "I find myself reflecting whimsically on how very much like the sagebrush the people are, at least in the hinterland that makes up most of Nevada, setting down their roots and thriving in unlikely places, hardy and resilient, stubborn and independent, restrained by environment and yet able to grow free."

Las Vegas, the city I have called home for five decades fits into Laxalt's definition. At the turn of the last century, its existence was due mostly to a railroad that ran between Los Angeles and Salt Lake City. However, the Nevadans Laxalt described so many years ago built Las Vegas into a destination resort where more than 35 million people from around the world come to play every year.

I salute author Guy Clifton with a few submissions collected from my years in Las Vegas:

You know you're a Nevadan if . . .
You had breakfast at Papa Gar's.
You went to The Flame to celebrate a big Rebel victory.
You can remember when Las Vegas Boulevard was known as Fifth Street.
You can remember when Sahara Boulevard was San Francisco Boulevard.
You cruised down Fremont Street as a teenager.
You had a hamburger and a shake at Sil's Drive-in at corner of Fifth and Charleston.
You could get from one end of town to the other in 10 minutes.

I thoroughly enjoyed this book, which has brought back many memories while at the same time taught me some new trivia about Nevada. By the time you finish, I'm sure you'll have a fresh list of definitions of your own about what it truly means to be a Nevadan.

You know you're a Nevadan if...

☐ You can properly pronounce Ely, Wabuska, Verdi, Denio and Beowawe.

☐ You remember those wacky television commercials for the Carson City auto dealers — Dan Flammer, Andy Butti, Al Rutledge and Archie Pozzi.

☐ You've owned a letterman's jacket, T-shirt, gym shorts or gym bag from The Sportsman.

☐ You watched the Edgar, High and Fly show at the Centennial Coliseum.

☐ You remember the afternoon movie hosted by Betty Stoddard.

☐ You know there are no horses or cows at the Mustang Ranch and no rabbits at the Cottontail.

☐ You still call the Reno Hilton "the MGM."

Betty Stoddard

☐ You voted for Paul Laxalt for Carson City District Attorney, Lt. Governor, Governor or U.S. Senator and you wanted to vote for him for President.

☐ You were in the stands for The Day of the Hawk, Snow Bowl I or Snow Bowl II.

☐ You've eaten an Awful Awful.

☐ You drove past Cave Rock Manny's gorilla.

☐ You've filled up at Two Stiffs Selling Gas.

☐ You've run over a jackrabbit.

☐ You've seen Virginia City's Fred Andreasen win a hand-drilling competition.

☐ You've seen state laws being made at Jack's Bar.

Paul Laxalt

☐ You know who Chet and Link are.

☐ You know what going to the "Wal'" means.

☐ You've thrown a rock down a mine shaft.

☐ You've had a chili-cheese omelet at Landrums at 2 a.m.

☐ You know what a mucker is.

☐ You've been stuck behind a Fallon farmer driving his tractor on Highway 50. (Or you were that Fallon farmer.)

☐ You've eaten at the Martin Hotel in Winnemucca.

☐ You've had to wait for a cow to cross the highway.

11

- [ ] You've been mentioned in a Rollan Melton column.

- [ ] You know what a "Heart o' Gold" is.

- [ ] Mills Lane has called you "Bubba" if you're a male or kissed your hand if you're a female.

- [ ] You can pronounce Yparraguirre.

- [ ] You've been to Jim Butler Days in Tonopah, Armed Forces Day in Hawthorne, Carson Valley Days in Gardnerville, the Sheepherder's Festival in Elko, the Denio Community Picnic, the Fallon Cantaloupe Festival or Gabbs Day. (If you've been to all of them, consider yourself a native.)

- [ ] You think of only one lake when someone says THE lake.

- [ ] You've signed the book at the top of Mount Rose.

- [ ] You drove on Interstate-80 east of Lovelock before there were speed limits.

- [ ] You love the smell of sagebrush in the rain.

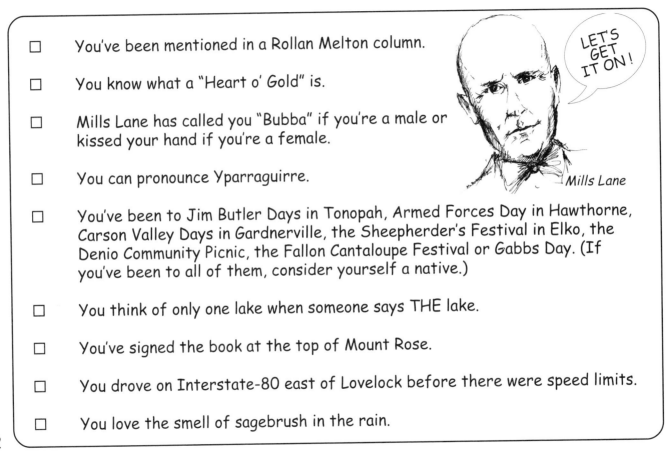

LET'S GET IT ON!

Mills Lane

☐   You've been to Jarbidge (not Jarbridge).

☐   You've used a piñon pine as a Christmas tree.

- ☐ You've fished the Ruby Marshes.

- ☐ You went to the hydroplane races at Pyramid Lake or Lake Tahoe.

- ☐ You went horseback riding or camping in the meadows of east Sparks.

- ☐ You've hunted ducks and fished for catfish at Washoe Lake.

- ☐ You've seen the biggest cutthroat of the season from Walker Lake hanging up in the El Cap.

- ☐ You've used turpentine to get the pitch off your hands after picking pine nuts.

- ☐ You've seen deer in the middle of the desert.

- ☐ You've made out on Windy Hill.

- ☐ You've driven through the Big Smoky Valley and fished at Kingston.

- ☐ You've floated Steamboat Ditch on an inner tube.

- ☐ You've floated the Truckee River on an inner tube.

- ☐ You remember when the only stoplight in Elko was at Fifth and Idaho streets.

- ☐ You've watched the "submarine races" at Soda Lake in Fallon.

- ☐ You rode a bike or motorcycle at the Plumb Lane or Seventh Street pits.

- ☐ You've seen pheasant in Yerington farm fields.

- ☐ You've gotten a speeding ticket near Goldfield.

- ☐ You've hunted greenhead at Greenhead.

- ☐ You've seen bighorn sheep on Mount Grant.

- [ ] You've seen a flock of mountain bluebirds in the central Nevada desert.

- [ ] You go up to Lake Tahoe, down to Las Vegas and over to Sacramento.

- [ ] You have used the term "In Stead of what?"

- [ ] You always loved to see Bertha and Tina — and, later, Angel.

- [ ] You remember the tree tunnel along Hash Lane before McCarran was a loop.

- [ ] You know it's Rattlesnake Mountain in Reno and Rattlesnake Hill in Fallon.

- [ ] You'll take the view from Mount Rose or Arc Dome over the view from any sky-scraper in America.

- [ ] You've simply been in awe of the view in Red Rock Canyon.

- [ ] You watched the Elko Arabs perform in a parade.

- [ ] You know U.S. 50 isn't even the loneliest road in Nevada, much less The Loneliest Road in America.

- [ ] You remember when Slide Mountain actually slid across U.S. 395 in Washoe Valley.

- [ ] You watched the jets dogfight and drop their bombs near Frenchman Flats.

- [ ] You've eaten at the Liberty Belle.

- [ ] You've seen the polar bear at Elko's Commercial Hotel.

- [ ] You know what an ichthyosaur is and have been to the park.

- [ ] You've had the prime rib at Sharkey's.

Sharkey

- [ ] You've been to the Carson Valley Country Club not for the golf, but for the grub.

- [ ] You voted for Dick Bryan for state assemblyman, state senator, attorney general, governor and U.S. Senator. (Throw in votes for him as Las Vegas High and University of Nevada student body president and consider yourself a native.)

- [ ] You get off an airplane anywhere else and say, "God, it's humid here."

- [ ] You simply referred to the namesake of McCarran Airport in Las Vegas and McCarran Boulevard in Reno and Sparks as "Pat."

Pat

- [ ] You know Moana (as in Lane, Stadium, etc.), is pronounced MO-ANN-A, not MO-ONN-A.

- [ ] You've eaten hot wings and pizza at the P.O. (Pizza Oven).

- [ ] You rode the mechanical bull at the Shy Clown.

□   You had the apple pie with butter sauce at Les Lerude's Wigwam restaurant.

19

☐ You remember shopping at Park Lane Mall in a blizzard... before it was an indoor mall.

☐ You bought your first skis at Codding & Wetzels or Mount Rose Sporting Goods.

☐ You got your neck scarf caught in the rope tow at Sky Tavern.

☐ You wash shorts and long johns in the same load of laundry.

☐ You watched jai alai at the MGM.

☐ You attended the John Denver Ski Classic.

☐ You've seen it snowing on the Fourth of July.

☐ You know it's time to plant your tomatoes when the snow is off Peavine.

☐ You remember Ormsby County.

☐ You sat in a neckers' seat with your sweetie at the Tower Theater . . . and . . . you remember where the Tower Theater was.

☐ You watched movies at the Granada, Tower, Crest or Majestic theaters.

☐ You've spent a sticky, hot, dusty, day gathering pine nuts after the first hard frost.

☐ You know Tree Green is a person and not a goal for Arbor Day.

☐ You've voted for Ugly Ed Feinhandler.

☐ You root for Andre Agassi.

☐ You remember Frankie Sue Del Papa driving her Mustang.

☐ Your favorite UNLV football player will always be Randall Cunningham even though the Ickey Shuffle was kind of cool.

☐ You've been stopped on U.S. 50 between Fallon and Austin by state trooper Banovich.

☐ You played tennis with Tilly Botti and he gave you some of his home-grown garlic.

☐ You've been bawled out by Smitty at Slide Mountain.

☐ You've heard Chris Talbot sing "American Pie" at the Beer Barrel.

Frankie Sue Del Papa

☐ You remember when Tennessee Ernie Ford was the choir director at the Lutheran church.

☐ You've seen a Tibaduiza win a running race.

☐ You listened to Cactus Tom on KOH.

☐ You either like Chris Ault or blame him for everything bad that has happened in the history of the state.

☐ You bought liquor from Ben.

☐ You remember when Tad Dunbar had a lot more hair and a lot less Tad.

☐ Jean Lukemberry or his daughter, Marie, served you a Picon punch at the J&T.

Tad Dunbar

☐ You took a journalism class from Higgy.

☐ You have a Robert Laxalt book, signed by the author.

☐ Tom Lilley was your weather man.

☐ You remember Joe Conforte giving away holiday turkeys before he became a federal fugitive.

☐ When you think of University of Nevada boxing, you think of Jimmie Olivas.

☐ You've met Bruno on a trip to the Black Rock.

☐ Jim Ellett, Lincoln Pike or Jack Rittenhouse refereed one of your high school games.

☐ You know who the Carson Crusher is.

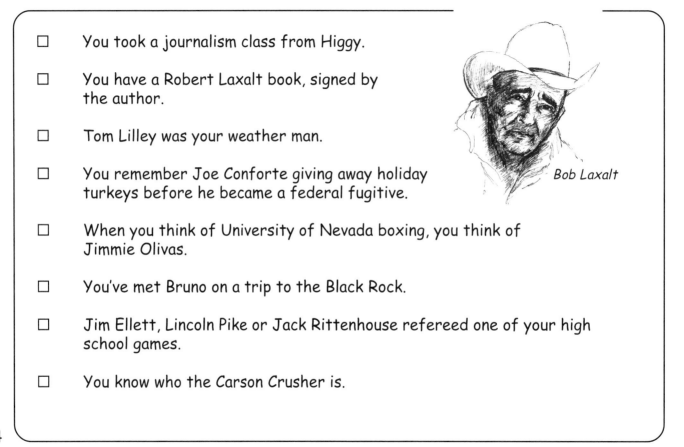

Bob Laxalt

- [ ] Pete Carruthers hosted a telethon that you watched and Jack Joseph a late-night TV movie.

- [ ] You've seen Glenn Lucky riding his bike between Carson City and Gardnerville.

- [ ] Marilyn Newton has taken your photo for the paper.

- [ ] Within radio range of Fallon, you listened to "the old bald-headed one" Ted Romero and the Country Caravan Show.

- [ ] You've been at a Nevada boxing match where Mills Lane received a louder ovation than the boxers.

- [ ] You've heard Bob Carroll's "Eye in the Sky" reports.

- [ ] You had the best doughnuts in the state at Spudnut.

Marilyn Newton

- ☐ You've seen "The Waver" (Ed Carlson) between Reno and Carson City — and made sure to wave back.

- ☐ You bought your first 45 and album from Mirabelli's.

- ☐ You've been represented in some capacity by Bill Raggio.

- ☐ You bought your first typewriter from Harry, Gordon or Gary Foote at Harry's Business Machines.

- ☐ You remember when Jack Joseph broadcast his radio show from the Waldorf Club.

- ☐ You never miss a John L. Smith column.

- ☐ You remember when Bob Carroll was news anchor at Channel 8 and Nick Laurie and Jerry Higgins were at Channel 4.

Ed Carlson

☐   You remember when schooners were a nickel at Beckers, free deli included.

☐   You want Bob Cashell or Don Manoukian to em-cee your event.

☐   You've seen one of the Marvel boys from Battle Mountain ride a buckin' horse.

☐   You had something printed by Harry Frost.

☐   You know Tark the Shark.

☐   You know Mary Ann (Dawn Wells) of Gilligan's Island is from Reno and was Miss Nevada.

☐   You watched Boss Hog play for the Wolf Pack.

Tark

☐ You've been serenaded by Pier Perrotti as he served you Italian food at Rivoli's.

☐ You know what it means to "swing and sweat with Tony Picetti."

☐ You remember the Primadonna girls.

☐ You parked in the middle of Maine Street in Fallon.

Pier Perrotti

☐ You went downtown to see the City of San Francisco come through.

☐ You were delivered by Dr. Noah Smernoff.

☐ You had take-out dinner from Bello's Tamales at Second and Washington.

☐ You've come home from a ski trip to Mount Rose more sunburned than after spending a day on the beach at Tahoe.

☐ You bought a pair of cowboy boots from Harry and Mush Parker.

☐ You remember 7-Up bottle cap day at the Majestic.

☐ You knew where people lived by the county designation on their blue plates.

☐ You're not at all surprised to see a tumbleweed stuck in someone's grill.

☐ You remember listening to Bob Chez on KOH radio. (You might be a native if you heard him on KELK.)

☐ You remember Pete Marich as the golf pro at Washoe.

☐ You've had Mama's raviolis at Casale's.

☐ You've ordered "A Mess" at the Coney Island.

☐ You bought toys from Uncle Happy.

☐ You can't help but like John Ascuaga.

☐ You went on a bus trip around the state with Jean Ford exploring Nevada women's history.

☐ You ate chocolate covered bumblebees, ants and caterpillars from Tony's Delicatessen and Tony personally handed you your sandwich.

☐ You remember going to the Picadilly on Virginia Street across from Harolds Club and they served Moscow Mules in fancy copper mugs.

☐ You remember going to Southworth's Cigar Store on Virginia Street near the railroad tracks and getting out-of-town newspapers.

☐ You remember when there was a mattress factory in the California Building.

John Ascuaga

☐ You had a custom cowboy hat made by Reno Hat Works on North Virginia Street.

☐ You ate at "The Big Hat" before it became "Two Guys From Italy," before it became "La Vecchia."

☐ You used to go into the old Rauhut's Bakery on Commercial Row, buy a loaf of just-baked cinnamon bread drizzled with icing, and eat it all yourself.

☐ You ice skated on the ponds at Idlewild Park and Manzanita Lake, and you can remember watching the firefighters hosing down the ice in the evening so it would be nice and slick for the skaters after the overnight freeze.

31

☐ You played in or watched the annual football game in Carson City on Admission Day between Reno and Carson high schools.
(If you took the V&T to the game,
consider yourself a native.)

☐ You saw the great Earl Dunn play basketball.

☐ You remember the burning of the fall leaves on the streets of Reno.

☐ You remember when street cars went down Virginia Street.

☐ You remember when Galletti Way was known as Coney Island Drive.

☐ You remember when Rancho San Rafael was called the Jensen Ranch.

Earl Dunn

☐ You remember when Levis were $2.35 a pair at Parker's Western Wear.

PARKERS

☐ You remember playing around the V&T bridge, hoping the train would come through.

☐ You remember when Kietzke Lane was a gravel road.

☐ You heard a craps dealer at Harolds Club yell just as he threw the dice, "I bet on the mouse!"

Pappy Smith of Harolds Club

☐ You bought your first tank of gas at Tommy's Texaco on California Avenue.

☐ You bought candy at Arch Drug before going to watch free kids' movies at Harolds Club movie theater in the Douglas Alley. On the way home from the movie you stopped at Ramos Drugs or Powell Drug on California Avenue for a genuine fountain soda.

☐ You bought your bicycle at Oden's Cyclery on East Fourth and Lake streets.

☐ You remember stopping at Wilson's Drug Store on First and Virginia for an ice cream cone.

☐ You read Joe Delaney's entertainment columns in the Las Vegas Sun.

☐ You ate baby burgers at the A&W on Oddie before McDonald's came to town.

☐ You know that McGill had a beanery — and it wasn't full of beans.

☐ You've been to a badger fight in McGill.

☐ You remember when May meant Helldorado Days in Las Vegas.

☐ You know that the Chicken Shack in Ely was not full of chickens.

☐ You ate Sunday brunch at the Painted Rock Café.

☐ You had a sundae from the Roaring '20s in Old Town Mall.

☐ You shopped at the Supply Sergeant across the tracks from downtown.

☐ You ate brains and eggs or Chili Mac from Kiah's Squeeze Inn.

Kiah

☐ You took tennis lessons from Alan Schute.

☐ You went to Bowers Mansion for school picnics, and swam to the island in the middle of the pool.

☐ You watched wrestling, magic shows and numerous community events at the State Building.

☐ You went to Cotillion class at the old Twentieth Century Club.

☐ You learned to swim at the old Moana pool and remember having to walk through the disinfecting puddle before getting in the pool.

☐ You ate at the Sun Café.

☐ You had pancakes at Uncle John's after mass at St. Thomas Cathedral.

☐ You remember the "jam sessions" that took place in the early morning hours at the Golden Hotel when some of the best musicians in the country finished their gigs at the big casinos and played just for fun.

☐ You can remember stopping for the train when cruising Virginia Street and swapping cars to ride with other friends; visiting with the pedestrian tourists crossing the street; and, if it was a long train, turning up the radio and dancing in the street.

☐ You remember when there was actually open space — lots of open space — between Las Vegas, Henderson and Boulder City.

☐ You remember when Boomtown was Bill and Effie's.

☐ You dove off the 40-foot and 20-foot towers at Lawton Springs swimming pool.

☐ You remember the Plymouth dealership at 777 S. Virginia, with Bud Moon and Frenchie Lavar doing their commercials.

☐ You remember "The Singing Cherokee."

☐ You still call Bill Ireland "Coach I."

☐ You remember Stampfli's Record Shop, downtown.

☐ You remember when you could go into abandoned mines in Virginia City.

☐ You remember Sundown Town, a Western amusement park off Joy Lake Road.

☐ You purchased your shoes at the Buster Brown Store on Virginia Street.

☐ You ate poolside at the Riverside Hotel.

Coach I

- [ ] You walked across Manzanita Lake on the wooden ice covered bridge.

- [ ] You looked in the steam-covered windows of the old Welch's Bakery and smelled the bread baking on Virginia St.

- [ ] You took time off from studying in the wee hours and went to the Cal-Neva for the 49-cent breakfast.

- [ ] Your Friday or Saturday nights weren't complete without several stops at the Cow Palace or the Frost Top.

- [ ] You remember the enormous golden rooster in front of the Nugget.

- [ ] You used to return from a weekend camping and arrowhead hunting by simply driving onto the pavement of highway 40 east of Sparks — and when I-80 was completed you found yourself blocked by a fence and had to backtrack 20 miles through the desert to take local roads into town.

- [ ] Dick Angelini was your scoutmaster.

☐ Marvel Guisti was your high school guidance counselor.

☐ Your prom was at the Mapes Skyroom.

☐ You often switch from "heat" to "A/C" in the same day.

☐ You remember the brick building on Second Street where Bill Harrah had the auto dealership for Rolls Royce, Ferrari, Aston Martin, and Lamborghini.

☐ You tore up your truck or car driving up to Hunter Lake (reservoir) from off Skyline.

☐ You've been stitched up in the emergency room by Senator Bernice Mathews.

☐ You floated down the old covered flue west of Reno and tried to avoid rusty nails.

☐ You remember the gas station on Fourth and Virginia where Rissoni was always fixing tires.

RENO'S **Mapes** MOTOR HOTEL

Bernice Mathews

☐ You remember red plastic drink tokes for free drinks at the casinos.

☐ You remember when the entire Reno City Council was Italian.

☐ Barbara Bennett was your favorite mayor.

☐ You remember Fat Boy's hamburger joint by Reno High School.

Barbara Bennett

☐ You remember when most people thought Lavere Redfield was a poor old bum, but when he died they had guards with shotguns loading the armored cars with all the silver dollars from the basement of his two story stone home on Mt. Rose Street.

☐ You remember when Fernley only had one stop light.

☐ You can remember swinging on the rope at the Moana swimming pool.

- ☐ You've cashed your paycheck at the Western Village just to get a free pull on a slot machine and two free drink tokes.

- ☐ Your Pop Warner football team was called the Greenbrae Packers.

- ☐ You frequented the Golden Bubble in Gardnerville before it became Sharkey's.

- ☐ You have never owned an umbrella — and never will.

- ☐ You know Governor Mike.

- ☐ You tip every bartender and cocktail waitress who serves you a drink.

- ☐ You bought an appliance from Landa, Linnecke, Lubra or Lusetti.

- ☐ You bought your groceries at Eagle-Thrifty or Sewell's.

Mike O'Callaghan

- [ ] You redeemed Model Dairy bottle caps for S&H Green Stamps at Grey Reid's.

- [ ] You swam at Reno Hot Springs, the "world's largest outdoor mineral hot springs."

- [ ] You watched the first Air Races at the Sky Ranch on Pyramid Lake Road.

- [ ] You ice skated at Burgess Field (courtesy of the Sparks Fire Department).

- [ ] You ate dinner at the Nevada Game Farm on Longley Lane.

- [ ] You ate family style dinners at the Toscano or Columbo hotels on Lake Street.

- [ ] You had dinner at the Winnemucca Hotel for $1 per person, Picons not included.

- [ ] You joined friends at the Mesa for dinner and a great view.

- [ ] You remember sidewalk elevators used for downtown deliveries.

- [ ] You remember the rings in the curb for tying horse reins at Parker's Western Wear at Second and Center.

- [ ] You danced at the El Patio Ballroom.

- [ ] You attended the Cow Pasture Boxing Festival.

- [ ] Max Corsun made you a sandwich and shared a story at Max C's in downtown Vegas.

- [ ] You had a cold one in the revolving Merry-Go-Round Bar on Second Street.

- [ ] You drove through the old lumber yards on West Fourth Street to go fishing on the Truckee.

- [ ] You remember when the Liberty Belle was called the Red Barn.

- [ ] You remember when the US 395 and Mount Rose Highway junction was controlled by a two-way stop sign. North-south traffic didn't have to stop at the intersection — only those on the Mount Rose or Virginia City highways did.

- [ ] You've had a Sierra Beer on the verandah of Pat Hart's Brass Rail Saloon.

- [ ] You remember the houses being moved from Vine Street to make way for I-80.

- [ ] You shopped at the Buffalo Trading Post.

- [ ] You used to go horseback riding at Baker Stables.

- [ ] You fogged up the car windows at the Midway Drive-in.

- [ ] You've run or walked the Journal Jog.

- [ ] You danced on Highway 395 in Gardnerville, when the highway was closed for the Carson Valley Days Street dance.

- [ ] You were on the Uncle Happy's Playhouse TV show back in the '50s.

- [ ] You remember when Vassar Street was the end of town.

- [ ] You walked on the silver dollars that were set in concrete in front of the Bank Club on Center Street.

- [ ] You have watched or participated in a basketball game involving the Stewart Indian School.

- [ ] You watched a football game at the old Mackay Stadium.

- [ ] You rode your bike to Woolworth's for a snow cone in the summer.

- [ ] You shopped for school supplies at Armanko's.

- [ ] You went ice skating at the Centennial Coliseum.

- [ ] You enjoyed the view, the spinach salad, the grapes in wine sauce at The Lancer and you remember when it burned down in 1971. Maybe you remember when it was the Mesa.

- [ ] You've gone to Mackay Stadium to sit on the field and watch fireworks on the Fourth of July.

- [ ] You remember the Lake Mansion before it was moved to Kietzke and South Virginia.

- [ ] You remember Jimmy Powell at the Bundox, then at the Sword Room, then Pepe's in the Eldorado, then upstairs to La Strada.

- [ ] You remember Herb Hallman Chevrolet.

- [ ] You had the baked Alaska at Chez Maxim on South Virginia.

- [ ] You remember the Christmas Tree and chef Gloria Michaels when she had her lions and tigers.

- [ ] You did your hardware shopping at Commercial Hardware.

- [ ] You remember Vario's.

- [ ] You shopped at Shim's Army Navy store.

- [ ] You got your paint from Wright's Paint on Keystone and Vine.

Commercial HARDWARE CO INC

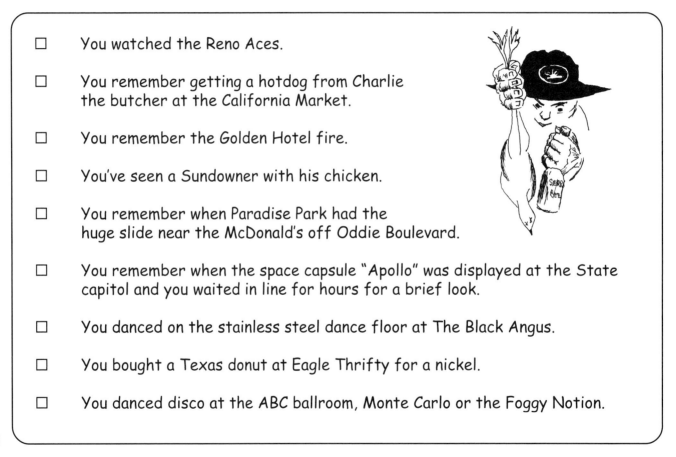

☐ You watched the Reno Aces.

☐ You remember getting a hotdog from Charlie the butcher at the California Market.

☐ You remember the Golden Hotel fire.

☐ You've seen a Sundowner with his chicken.

☐ You remember when Paradise Park had the huge slide near the McDonald's off Oddie Boulevard.

☐ You remember when the space capsule "Apollo" was displayed at the State capitol and you waited in line for hours for a brief look.

☐ You danced on the stainless steel dance floor at The Black Angus.

☐ You bought a Texas donut at Eagle Thrifty for a nickel.

☐ You danced disco at the ABC ballroom, Monte Carlo or the Foggy Notion.

☐ You remember the "old strip" in Las Vegas — and you miss it.

☐ You stopped at the Mayfair Market for beverages before cruising Virginia Street.

☐ You've been given the shaft at Sheep Dip.

☐ You've eaten a Jimmy's submarine sandwich.

☐ You've dragged main for hours in Carson City from the Carousel Drive-In to the A&W.

☐ You've been to Hidden Beach back when people wore clothes there.

☐ You've been stuck on the road to Knot Creek Reservoir.

☐ You know the nickname of the sports teams at Gabbs High School.

☐ You've danced in the ballroom of the Austin Hotel.

☐ You've seen the cotton fields of Pahrump.

☐ You've been to Stokes Castle.

☐ You know the first city in Nevada to have headliner entertainers was Elko.

☐ You've had a steak at the Circle RB.

☐ You've watched a parade in downtown Reno.

☐ You've seen at least three versions of the Reno Arch.

☐ You remember when the main event at the Genoa Candy Dance really was a dance.

☐ You've watched the sunrise light up silvery sagebrush when pogonip has covered it with frost.

☐ You remember when Idlewild had the CCC Camp, a zoo and buffalos.

☐ You remember when the *Nevada State Journal* or the *Reno Evening Gazette* was delivered on the porch for a quarter a week.

☐ You remember that Grey Reid Wright's boxes were pink and maroon.

☐ You remember when City Hall was across the street from the Majestic.

☐ You remember when Baker had Lehman Caves but no motels.

☐ You remember when Dat-So-La-Lee baskets and white doeskin gloves were common.

☐ You remember when a Carson City dollar was only worth a buck.

Dat-So-La-Lee

☐ You remember when Arlington Avenue was Chestnut Street and the Dominican Nuns ran Saint Mary's Hospital.

☐ You remember when the road to Sacramento (US 40) was two lanes.

☐ You still call the Flamingo Hilton "The Primm."

☐ You remember the annual Tombolla festival.

☐ You remember the elephant foot ashtray at The Sportsman.

☐ You know the words to "Home Means Nevada." (See last page of book)

☐ You remember the Black Mariah driving through Reno during the Rodeo "arresting" anyone not in western clothes.

☐ You remember playing on the Fighter Jet at Kiddie Land in Idlewild Park.

Sister Seraphine of Saint Mary's

☐ You're either loyal to the Santa Fe or Louie's Basque Corner, but usually not both.

BASQUE FAMILY STYLE DINNERS

☐ You remember the Polynesian brunch at Harvey's Top of the Wheel.

☐ You watched the Silver Sox play.

☐ You remember Herb Foster, John Robb and Tip Whitehead as people, not football fields and Jake Lawlor as a coach, not an events center.

☐ You had lunch at the Bundox Restaurant and ice cream at the soda fountain across the street in Cerveri drugstore.

☐ You remember when there were only channels 2, 4 and 8 in Reno.

☐ You remember when the Peppermill was a little coffee shop and the Atlantis was the Golden Door.

Jake Lawlor

☐ You remember when Old Town Mall really tried to look like an old western town.

☐ You and your friends met at the Q-ne-Q, O'Brien's, Lee's Drive-In, Ray's Drive-In or Penguins.

☐ You went sledding at Washoe golf course in winter.

☐ You had dinner at Spaughi's and remember the dripping candles on the old wine bottles on every table.

☐ You remember the peacocks at Arlington Gardens nursery.

☐ You had Model Dairy deliver to your door.

☐ You marveled at the "ultra modern" space-age architecture of Century 21 theaters.

☐ You watched Laurel and Hardy at Straw Hat Pizza at Shoppers Square and then had ice cream next door at Blum's.

☐ You know "Machine Gun" Thompson and "Spiderman" Burns are Las Vegas legends, but not as gangsters.

☐ You know Nevada's Ty Cobb was a newsman, not a baseball player.

☐ You played on the steam engine outside the Nevada State Museum in Carson City.

☐ You've seen the Rat Pack at the Sands in Las Vegas.

Ty Cobb

☐ You've convinced a tourist that jackalopes really do exist.

☐ You've been to Sand Mountain and still have little bits of sand in your shoes, clothes, vehicle, etc.

☐ You've stopped at Bob's Root Beer in Fallon after a day at Lahontan.

- [ ] You can't name the Las Vegas City Council, but you can name the starting five for the Runnin' Rebels national championship basketball team — Larry Johnson, Stacy Augmon, Greg Anthony, Anderson Hunt and David Butler. (If you can name half of the "Hard Way Eight," consider yourself a native.)

- [ ] You remember the New Penny Singers, the Sierra Boys Choir, and the Reno Civic Chorus.

- [ ] You remember buying penny candy at Hale's Drug Store on the corner of Fourth and Vine.

- [ ] Carmel Caruso taught you how to play craps.

- [ ] You remember when Keystone Avenue was called Peavine Road.

Carmel Caruso

- [ ] You remember Chism Ice Cream.

- [ ] You know where and what the Bullhead is.

- ☐ You ate lunch or dinner at Molly's Fish & Chips.

- ☐ You've had a Big Mac from a Luther Mack-owned McDonald's.

- ☐ You used to go pine nut gathering and stop to "roast" them in Steamboat hot springs on the way home.

- ☐ You remember the old Dayton Valley Inn when it was still called The International.

- ☐ You bought your new school wardrobe at Grey Reid's.

- ☐ Bud Beasley has taught you or coached you.

- ☐ You've attended the Fathers' Day Picnic in Paradise Valley.

- ☐ You've had a milkshake or a phosphate at Bay's Fountain in Eureka.

Bud Beasley

- ☐ You remember Blanchard, Hubbard and Boeing fields.

☐   You still call it Boulder Dam.

Home Means Nevada
Words and Music by Bertha Raffetto

Way out in the land of the setting sun,
Where the wind blows wild and free,
There's a lovely spot, just the only one
That means home sweet home to me.
If you follow the old Kit Carson trail,
Until desert meets the hills,
Oh you certainly will agree with me,
It's the place of a thousand thrills.

Home means Nevada
Home means the hills,
Home means the sage and the pines.
Out by the Truckee's silvery rills,
Out where the sun always shines,
There is the land that I love the best,
Fairer than all I can see.
Right in the heart of the golden west
Home means Nevada to me.

Whenever the sun at the close of day,
Colors all the western sky,
Oh my heart returns to the desert grey
And the mountains tow'ring high.
Where the moon beams play in shadowed glen,
With the spotted fawn and doe,
All the live long night until morning light,
Is the loveliest place I know.

Home means Nevada
Home means the hills,
Home means the sage and the pines.
Out by the Truckee's silvery rills,
Out where the sun always shines,
There is the land that I love the best,
Fairer than all I can see.
Right in the heart of the golden west
Home means Nevada to me.